Under My Feet

Chipmunks

Patricia Whitehouse

Heinemann Library
Chicago, Illinois

j599.364
WHI

© 2004 Heinemann Library
a division of Reed Elsevier Inc.
Chicago, Illinois

Customer Service 888-454-2279
Visit our website at www.heinemannlibrary.com

All rights reserved. No part of this publication may be reproduced or transmitted in any form or by any means, electronic or mechanical, including photocopying, recording, taping, or any information storage and retrieval system, without permission in writing from the publisher.

Designed by Sue Emerson, Heinemann Library; Page layout by Que-Net Media™
Printed and bound in the United States by Lake Book Manufacturing, Inc.
Photo research by Bill Broyles

08 07 06 05 04
10 9 8 7 6 5 4 3 2 1

Library of Congress Cataloging-in-Publication Data
Whitehouse, Patricia, 1958-
    Chipmunks / Patricia Whitehouse.
        v. cm. – (Under my feet)
Contents: Do chipmunks live here? – What are chipmunks? – What do chipmunks look like? – Where do chipmunks live? – What do chipmunk homes look like? – How do chipmunks find their way underground? – How do chipmunks make their homes? – What is special about chipmunk homes? – When do chipmunks come out from underground? – Chipmunk home map.
    ISBN 1-4034-4319-X (HC), 1-4034-4328-9 (Pbk.)
    1. Chipmunks–Juvenile literature. [1. Chipmunks.] I. Title.
    QL737.R68W377 2003
    599.36'4–dc21

                              2003000036

Acknowledgments
The author and publishers are grateful to the following for permission to reproduce copyright material:
p. 4 Suzanne Szasz/Photo Researchers, Inc.; pp. 5, 12, 13, 20 Dwight Kuhn; p. 6 William J. Weber/Visuals Unlimited; pp. 7, 14 Tom McHugh/Photo Researchers, Inc.; p. 8 Kim Taylor/Bruce Coleman Inc.; p. 9 Jack Ballard/Visuals Unlimited; p. 10 S. Maslowski/Visuals Unlimited; p. 11 Rich Kirchner/NHPA; p. 15 Joe DiStetens/Photo Researchers, Inc.; p. 16 David S. Addison/Visuals Unlimited; p. 17 Tom & Pat Leeson/Photo Researchers, Inc.; p. 18 Stephen J. Krasemann/DRK Photo; p. 19 Leonard Lee Rue III/Leonard Rue Enterprises; p. 21 Gregory K. Scott/Photo Researchers, Inc.; p. 23 (row 1, L-R) Tom & Pat Leeson/Photo Researchers, Inc., Tom McHugh/Photo Researchers, Inc., William J. Weber/Visuals Unlimited; (row 2, L-R) S. Maslowski/Visuals Unlimited, Dwight Kuhn, Tom McHugh/Photo Researchers, Inc.; (row 3) Dwight Kuhn; back cover Tom McHugh/Photo Researchers, Inc.

Illustration on page 22 by Will Hobbs
Cover photograph by John Mitchell/Photo Researchers, Inc.

Every effort has been made to contact copyright holders of any material reproduced in this book. Any omissions will be rectified in subsequent printings if notice is given to the publisher.

Special thanks to our advisory panel for their help in the preparation of this book:

Alice Bethke, Library Consultant
Palo Alto, CA

Eileen Day, Preschool Teacher
Chicago, IL

Kathleen Gilbert,
Second Grade Teacher
Round Rock, TX

Sandra Gilbert,
Library Media Specialist
Fiest Elementary School
Houston, TX

Jan Gobeille,
Kindergarten Teacher
Garfield Elementary
Oakland, CA

Angela Leeper,
Educational Consultant
Wake Forest, NC

Special thanks to Mark Rosenthal, Abra Prentice Wilkin Curator of Large Mammals at Chicago's Lincoln Park Zoo, for his help in the preparation of this book.

Some words are shown in bold, **like this.**
You can find them in the picture glossary on page 23.

Contents

Do Chipmunks Live Here?

When you walk outside, you might not see a chipmunk.

But you might be walking over one.

Chipmunks live under your feet.

Their homes are underground.

What Are Chipmunks?

Chipmunks are **rodents**.

Chipmunks and other rodents are **mammals**.

Mammals have fur or hair.

Mammals make milk for their babies.

What Do Chipmunks Look Like?

tail   toe

A chipmunk has four legs and a long, furry tail.

It has five toes on each paw.

It has dark and light stripes on its back.

Chipmunks are about the size of a mouse.

Where Do Chipmunks Live?

Chipmunks live alone in an underground home.

A chipmunk's home is called a **burrow**.

Chipmunks live where trees grow.

Some chipmunks live in city parks.

What Do Chipmunk Homes Look Like?

A **burrow** has a **nest**.

Nests are filled with soft grass or leaves.

Some burrows have rooms
called **chambers.**

Chipmunks put food in
the chambers.

How Do They Find Their Way?

Chipmunks use their eyes to see underground.

Some light comes into their **tunnels** during the day.

Chipmunks use their noses.

They can smell food they hide underground.

How Do Chipmunks Make Their Homes?

Some chipmunks dig **burrows** with their front paws.

They push the dirt out with their nose and front paws.

Other chipmunks move into empty burrows.

These burrows were made by other animals, like this **badger**.

What Is Special About Their Homes?

Chipmunks hide the holes to their **burrows**.

The holes are near rocks or plants.

Most burrows have many ways to get in.

This helps chipmunks get away from danger quickly.

When Do Chipmunks Come Out from Underground?

When it is warm, chipmunks leave their **burrows** to find food.

They go back at night to sleep.

Chipmunks sleep most of the winter.

They might leave their burrows if it is not too cold.

Chipmunk Home Map

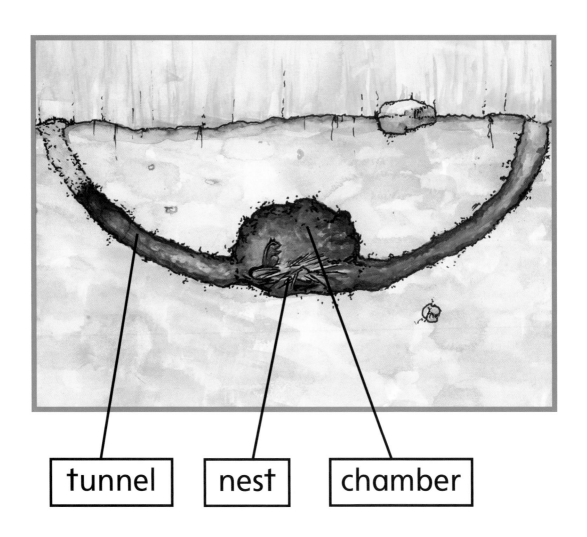

tunnel nest chamber

Picture Glossary

badger
page 17

mammal
pages 6, 7

rodent
page 6

burrow
pages 10, 12,
13, 16, 17, 18,
19, 20, 21

nest
pages 12, 22

tunnel
pages 14, 22

chamber
pages 13, 22

Note to Parents and Teachers

Reading for information is an important part of a child's literacy development. Learning begins with a question about something. Help children think of themselves as investigators and researchers by encouraging their questions about the world around them. Each chapter in this book begins with a question. Read the question together. Look at the pictures. Talk about what you think the answer might be. Then read the text to find out if your predictions were correct. Think of other questions you could ask about the topic, and discuss where you might find the answers. Assist children in using the picture glossary and the index to practice new vocabulary and research skills.

 CAUTION: Remind children that it is not a good idea to handle wild animals or insects. Children should wash their hands with soap and water after they touch any animal.

Index